The Art of Less

Minimalism of Mind, Space and Heart

JRA

Chapter 1: Introduction to Minimalism

Minimalism is an approach to living that focuses on reducing the non-essentials in order to focus on what has significant value. Originating as an art movement in the 20th century, minimalism has evolved into a philosophy of life that promotes simplicity and clarity.

This lifestyle aims to eliminate excess, simplifying one's possessions and reducing commitments. The goal is to create space for greater mental clarity, creativity, and inner satisfaction. By reducing the possession of material objects and focusing on experiences, a sense of freedom and well-being can be achieved.

The history of the minimalist movement has its roots in the art world, where artists such as Donald Judd and Dan Flavin have adopted a simple and essential style. This aesthetic then spread into everyday life, becoming an approach to life that embraces simplicity and functionality.

Living with less offers significant benefits. Reducing the consumption and possession of material goods can lead to greater financial freedom and a decrease in the stress associated with hoarding possessions. Additionally, minimalism fosters deeper relationships, as the focus shifts from things to people. This lifestyle can also help reduce your environmental impact, as you consume fewer resources and produce less waste.

Minimalism is an approach that seeks to simplify life by focusing on the essential value. Through reducing excess and focusing on the meaningful, greater satisfaction, richer relationships, and a positive impact on the environment can be achieved.

Here are the benefits of minimalism:

Financial freedom: By reducing consumption and having fewer material goods, space is freed up in the budget and financial resources can be allocated to things that really matter, such as travel, experiences and investments. Minimalism offers a unique opportunity to achieve financial freedom, freeing yourself from the constraints of consumerism and the accumulation of superfluous objects.

When you adopt a minimalist lifestyle, you become more aware of your priorities and learn to distinguish between what's really important and what's just a temporary desire. This allows you to reduce unnecessary expenses and concentrate financial resources on what brings lasting value to your life.

One of the main consequences of minimalism is the ability to save money. Owning fewer items means spending less on purchase, maintenance and storage space. Furthermore, by reducing consumption, recurring expenses associated with superfluous consumer goods are also reduced. This money saved can be used for things that really matter, such as travel, experiences and investments.

The financial freedom that comes through minimalism is not just about being able to buy what you want, but also about the freedom to choose how you want to live your life. With fewer financial worries and fewer ties to consumerism, you can spend more time and energy on what you truly love, such as pursuing your passions, spending time with loved ones, or pursuing personal goals.

Greater Mental Clarity: By eliminating clutter and overloaded objects, you create more mental space to focus on what's really important, reducing stress and anxiety. Minimalism isn't just about physical appearance, it also has a significant impact on our mind and psychological well-being.

Living in an orderly environment free from visual distractions allows the mind to relax and focus on what's really important. When the number of objects around us is reduced, the mental load associated with their management and maintenance is also reduced. This leads to greater mental clarity and a feeling of lightness.

Minimalism invites us to reflect on our true priorities and to focus on what makes us happy and fulfilled. By eliminating superfluous objects, space is created for the things that really matter in our lives, such as relationships, passions and meaningful experiences. This allows us to live more authentically and to devote our time and energy to what makes us feel truly fulfilled.

Furthermore, minimalism helps us to free ourselves from the stress and anxiety associated with owning and hoarding objects. Often, the desire to have more and more can lead to a constant search for external satisfaction, which ultimately turns out to be empty and unsatisfying. Breaking free from this cycle of craving and dissatisfaction allows us to find inner peace and focus on the things that truly make us happy.

The clarity of mind that comes through minimalism allows us to make more informed decisions and live more intentionally. It helps us focus on the present, enjoy what we have and not let ourselves be distracted by what is superfluous. This leads us to greater satisfaction and greater serenity in our daily lives.

Deeper Relationships: By focusing on people rather than possessing objects, one can develop a greater connection with others, strengthening relationships and creating meaningful moments together. Minimalism invites us to shift attention from material goods to the people around us, paving the way for more authentic and profound relationships.

When we free ourselves from attachment and dependence on objects, we are able to devote more time and energy to the people we love. Possessing fewer objects means having fewer distractions and more room for meaningful relationships. This allows us to create precious moments together, to share experiences and to deepen the connection with others.

Minimalism encourages us to value the quality of our relationships, rather than the quantity.

It pushes us to focus on the people who inspire, support and enrich us, eliminating toxic or superficial relationships. This allows us to create a space for the people who truly matter in our lives and to develop more authentic and meaningful connections.

Also, minimalism helps us reduce stress and tension in relationships. When we free ourselves from the hoarding of possessions and the desire to have more and more, we are able to focus on the true needs of the people we love. This allows us to be more present, empathetic and available, creating an environment of trust and mutual support. Minimalism also invites us to experience moments of sharing and generosity. Having fewer objects means having more resources to share with others.

We can devote our time, skills and financial resources to supporting the people we love and contributing to the well-being of the community in which we live. This allows us to create a positive impact in the lives of others and to build relationships based on reciprocity and solidarity.

Minimalism offers the opportunity to develop deeper and more meaningful relationships. By focusing on people rather than possessions, we can create precious moments together, strengthen connections, and experience greater satisfaction in our relationships. Minimalism invites us to evaluate the quality of our relationships, to reduce stress and tension and to experience moments of sharing and generosity.

Climate change is one of the most pressing challenges facing humanity. Reducing our environmental impact therefore becomes a crucial aspect of preserving our planet for future generations.

Adopting a minimalist lifestyle can help reduce your greenhouse gas emissions and overall carbon footprint. Owning fewer objects means consuming fewer natural resources, reducing the production of waste and the use of energy. Furthermore, by reducing the consumption of superfluous consumer goods, the demand for industrial production is also reduced, which is often responsible for high greenhouse gas emissions.

Furthermore, a minimalist lifestyle also encourages the adoption of sustainable practices, such as the use of renewable energy, recycling and reducing food waste. These actions help mitigate climate change and preserve our planet's natural resources.

Focus on Internal Satisfaction: With fewer material distractions, you focus more on personal experiences and your own inner well-being, leading to greater overall satisfaction. Minimalism invites us to reflect on our true priorities and to devote time and energy to what makes us truly happy.

When we free ourselves from the attachment to objects and social conventions that drive us to seek happiness in material possessions, we discover that true satisfaction comes from within us. We realize that experiences, meaningful relationships and personal development are what truly nourishes us and makes us feel fulfilled. Minimalism encourages us to pause and evaluate what truly makes us happy.

We eliminate what we don't need, we focus on what brings us joy and satisfaction. This can mean spending more time on the passions and interests we are passionate about, cultivating meaningful relationships with the people we love, and investing in our personal and spiritual growth.

When we focus on internal satisfaction instead of material things, we discover a deeper and more lasting joy. Happiness is no longer linked to the purchase of objects, but it is a feeling that arises from alignment with our values, gratitude for what we have and awareness of the present moment.

The philosophy of minimalism is based on the search for **simplicity and clarity** in everyday life. Living with fewer material objects and reducing superfluous commitments allows you to simplify life, freeing up mental and energy space for what is really important. Without the burden of unnecessary things, it becomes easier to make quick and informed decisions, act efficiently and focus on activities that bring value and satisfaction. The reduction of the complexity of daily processes leads to greater tranquility and harmony, allowing you to fully enjoy experiences and relationships without unnecessary distractions. Minimalism invites us to reflect on our priorities and eliminate what does not contribute to our well-being, paving the way for a more authentic and meaningful life.

The practice of minimalism can have a significant impact on our creativity. By freeing ourselves from excesses and distractions, we create a mental and physical space that favors the emergence of new ideas and meaningful projects. When we focus on what truly matters, we are able to explore our passions and interests in a more profound and authentic way. Reducing noise and clutter in our lives allows us to experience greater mental clarity, which in turn stimulates creativity. Without the pressure of having to deal with too many things or commitments, we are free to explore new avenues, to think more original and to find innovative solutions to problems we encounter along the way. Minimalism invites us to free our mind and space, opening the door to a freer and more inspired creative flow.

Minimalism is the art
of eliminating the
superfluous and
embracing the essential.

Chapter 2: Simplifying Physical Space

Simplifying the physical space is a key step on the path to minimalism. Here are some explanations on how to de-clutter and organize domestic spaces:

Evaluating Objects: Start by evaluating each object in your home. Ask yourself if you really need that item and if it brings you joy or utility. If not, consider donating, recycling, or throwing it away. Evaluating objects is a fundamental step on the path to minimalism. Take the time to carefully examine each item in your home and reflect on its value in your life. Genuinely ask yourself if you really need that item or if you could do without it.

If the item doesn't evoke any positive emotions in you or if you haven't used it for a long time, it may be time to part with it.

There are several options available for getting rid of items you no longer need. You may consider **donating** them to charities or people in need. That way, your items can find a new home and you can contribute to a worthy cause.

If the item is no longer usable or can't be donated, you can consider recycling. Make sure you follow your local guidelines for proper recycling of materials.

In some cases, it may be necessary to simply discard the item. However, try to minimize the amount of waste you produce, always favoring recycling or donating whenever possible.

Remember that the process of evaluating items can take time and thought. Don't be in a hurry to make decisions, but be determined in pursuing your goal of living in a more minimalist way. Over time, getting rid of superfluous objects will allow you to create a more orderly and harmonious space, while also freeing your mind from unnecessary distractions.

One area at a time: An effective approach to approach the decluttering process is to focus on one area at a time. This will help you avoid feeling overwhelmed and will allow you to give each area proper attention and care.
You can start by selecting a single closet, a room, or a specific category of items. For example, you might decide to start with clothing, books, or kitchen utensils.

Pick the area that you feel you can tackle most easily or that you think is the messiest. Once the area is selected, take the time to examine each item within it. Evaluate whether that item is truly useful to you or if it brings you joy. If the answer is no, consider parting with it.

You can use different criteria to make informed decisions. For example, you might ask yourself if you've used that item in the past six months or if you plan to use it in the future. If the answer is no, it might be time to get rid of it.

During the process, keep in mind the goal of living more minimalistic. Ask yourself how each item fits into your lifestyle and if it contributes to your overall well-being.

Remember that minimalism is not just about eliminating unnecessary items, but also about putting an emphasis on quality and awareness of what you own.

Tackling one area at a time will allow you to stay focused and see tangible progress on your path to minimalism. Once you've completed one area, you can move on to the next, continuing to get rid of items you no longer need and creating a more orderly and harmonious space around you.

Rule of "less is more: The rule of "less is more" is a fundamental principle of minimalism. The goal is to keep only the objects that are truly useful or that bring you joy in your daily life.
A good practice is to get rid of duplicate objects. We often accumulate more than one similar item without realizing it, such as several pairs of scissors or coffee mugs. Carefully consider whether you really need more of a similar item, and if not, consider donating or selling the extras.

Consider items you haven't touched in months. If an item has been forgotten in a corner of your home and you haven't used or thought about it for a long time, it could be a sign that you don't need it. Getting rid of them will allow you to free up space and simplify your life.

During the process of evaluating items, ask yourself if each item brings you joy. Minimalism is not only about eliminating superfluous objects, but also an emphasis on quality and awareness of what you own. Only keep items that make you happy, inspire you, or are truly useful to you.

Remember that minimalism is a personal journey and that there is no hard and fast rule about how many items you should own. The important thing is that every item you choose to keep has significant value in your life.

Getting rid of useless objects will allow you to create a tidier and more harmonious space, reducing stress and increasing your overall well-being.

Organizing in a functional way: Organizing in a functional way is a key element in maintaining a minimalist and tidy environment. Assigning a specific place to each item based on its function will help you find things more easily and maintain order over time.
Start by identifying the different categories of items you own, such as clothing, books, kitchen utensils, and so on. Next, give each category a dedicated space in your home. For example, you could dedicate a specific wardrobe or chest of drawers for clothing, a bookcase for books and a drawer for kitchen utensils.

Once you've assigned a space to each category, take the time to organize the items within it in a logical and functional way. For example, you can sort clothing by type (shirts, pants, party dresses) or by season. For books, you can organize them by genre or by author.

Use bins or boxes to keep similar items together and to keep them from scattering. Label containers clearly to make it easier to find the items you want.

As you organize, also consider how often items are used. Place the items you use most often in easily accessible places, while the less used items can be placed in less accessible areas or in storage spaces. Maintaining order requires consistency and discipline.

Make sure you store items in their designated place after using them and avoid hoarding items in undesignated areas. This will help you maintain order over time and enjoy the benefits of a minimalist and functional environment.

Minimize decoration: Minimal decoration is an important aspect of minimalism. Instead of overloading spaces with useless decorative items, it's wise to choose a few items that have personal meaning to you.
When it comes to decorating, quality is more important than quantity. Choose items that inspire you, make you feel happy, or have emotional value to you. These items can be photographs, artwork, handicrafts, or travel souvenirs. Make sure every decorative item has a purpose and a story that connects you to it.

Avoid overloading spaces with excessive decorative items. Leave space for light and circulating air, so the space feels open and relaxed. This will promote a feeling of cleanliness and visual order, creating a more harmonious environment.

Also, consider using functional decorative elements. For example, you can use plants to add a touch of greenery and vitality to spaces, as well as improve air quality. Choose furniture that is both aesthetically pleasing and functional, in order to optimize the available space.

Remember that minimalism does not mean depriving yourself of all forms of decoration, but rather carefully selecting the objects that add value and meaning to your life. Reducing the decoration will allow you to better appreciate the objects you have chosen to keep, creating a cleaner, more orderly and harmonious environment around you.

Storage Solutions: Storage solutions are essential tools for maintaining a minimalistic and organized environment. By using boxes, baskets and shelves, you can keep items organized and easily accessible when you need them.

Boxes are especially useful for storing items that are not used regularly. You can choose transparent boxes to have an immediate view of their contents or colored boxes to add a touch of style. Make sure you label the boxes clearly, indicating the contents, so you can find what you need more easily.

Baskets can be used to organize smaller items or to separate items within a drawer or cabinet. For example, you can use baskets to store household accessories, personal care products, or kitchen utensils.

This will allow you to keep items grouped together and prevent them from scattering. Shelves are a great way to take advantage of vertical space. You can use shelves to store books, decorative items, or other items you want to keep on display. Make sure you arrange items neatly and leave space between them to create a clean, harmonious look.

In addition to using storage solutions, it is also important to evaluate the amount of items you own. Reducing the number of items will allow you to have more space available and simplify the archiving process. Remember that minimalism is all about the essentials, so try to keep only items that are truly useful or bring you joy, and storage solutions should be tailored to your needs and your available space.

Experiment with different options and find the ones that work best for you. The goal is to create an orderly and functional space, where objects are easily accessible and where a sense of calm and serenity can flow.

Do a regular review: Doing a regular review is an important step on the path to minimalism. Even if you have already made an initial selection of items, it is normal that over time new items may accumulate or your needs may change.
Take time regularly to review spaces in your home and assess if there are any items you can still get rid of or rearrange. This will allow you to maintain a minimalist lifestyle and prevent unnecessary items from accumulating again.

During the review, ask yourself if the items you own continue to be useful or bring you joy. If an item no longer answers these questions, consider parting with it. You can donate it, sell it or recycle it, depending on its condition and your preferences.

Also, consider whether there are any areas of your home that could benefit from a rearrangement. You may find that some items can be moved to new locations to optimize space or to create a more functional environment. For example, you might decide to rearrange your bookshelves to fit a new sort order or move your cooking utensils to a more accessible drawer. Periodic review allows you to maintain control over the objects you own and to adapt your space to your current needs. It also helps you maintain a minimalist lifestyle over the long term by preventing unnecessary items from piling up again.

Build a List: Before you shop, make a detailed list of what you actually need. Stick to this list and try not to deviate from your goals. This simple exercise will help you avoid impulse buying and focus only on what's essential to you. When creating the list, take the time to reflect on your real needs and desires, avoiding being influenced by advertising or current trends. Ask yourself if the item you're considering buying will actually contribute to your long-term happiness and well-being. Often, we realize that much of what we thought we wanted is not really essential to our daily lives. Once you've created the list, commit yourself to following it closely.

This will allow you to save time, money and energy, as well as reduce the stress associated with accumulating unnecessary items. Remember that minimalism isn't just about physically eliminating the unnecessary, it's also about reducing distractions and optimizing your resources.

Set a budget: Set a spending limit for each purchase or for each period, such as the week or month. Keeping track of your expenses helps you avoid going over budget. When adopting a minimalist lifestyle, it's important to be aware of your finances and set clear limits on spending. This will allow you to maintain accurate control over your finances and avoid falling into the trap of consumerism and impulsive buying.

To establish an effective budget, start by analyzing your monthly income and expenses. Identify expense items that can be reduced or eliminated completely.

For example, you might want to cut back on meals out or subscriptions you don't use regularly. Once you've established a realistic budget, commit yourself to sticking to it.

A helpful strategy for keeping control of your spending is to keep track of every purchase you make. You can use an app or a simple spreadsheet to log your daily expenses. This will allow you to clearly see where your money is going and identify any areas where you can save further.

Here are some shopping rules:

Wait Before You Buy: Before making an impulsive purchase, take some time to think. Wait at least 24 hours before confirming the purchase. Often, after some time, you'll figure out if you really need that item.

Ask Critical Questions: Ask yourself if the item is really needed or if it can be replaced by something you already own. Also consider whether the purchase will contribute to your long-term well-being or if it's just a momentary gratification.

Avoid temptations: Limit situations that lead you to make impulse purchases. For example, avoid visiting online or physical stores when you are bored or emotionally unstable.

Pay with cash: Whenever possible, pay with cash instead of credit cards. Physically feeling the amount you're spending can help you be more aware of your purchasing choices.

Focus on quality: Invest in good quality items that will last over time, rather than opting for cheap but poor quality items that may need to be replaced soon.

Avoid flash sales: Temporary sales or flash deals can lead to impulse buying. Consider whether you would have bought that item at full price anyway.

Remember your financial goals: Always keep your long-term financial goals in mind, such as saving up for a vacation or investing in a project.

This rules can help you stay motivated to avoid impulse buys.

The more you have, the more you have to worry about. Minimalism frees the mind from the shackles of excess.

Chapter 3: Clearing Your Mind: Techniques for Creating Mental Space for the Important Stuff

Define your priorities. Identify the most important things in your life and focus on them, avoiding wasting energy on insignificant details. One of the fundamental keys to minimalism is having clear priorities in your life. This means taking the time to reflect on the things that are truly important to you and focus on them. Identifying your priorities will help you avoid wasting energy on insignificant details that can distract you from your main goal.

To set your priorities, you might start by making a list of the things that bring you the most joy and satisfaction in life.

These could be significant relationships, your career, leisure or your personal well-being. Once you've identified these areas, you can focus your attention and resources on them, eliminating distractions and activities that don't contribute to your overall well-being. Remember that minimalism is not just about eliminating material things, but also about simplifying your life in general. Focusing on priorities will help you make more informed decisions about how to spend your time, resources, and energy. This will allow you to live a more meaningful life, free from distractions and in line with your deepest values.

Don't try to handle everything on your own. Delegate tasks when possible and ask for help when you need it, freeing up mental space for what matters most. Another crucial aspect of minimalism is learning to delegate and ask for help when needed. Often, we try to handle everything ourselves, thinking it's a sign of strength or independence. However, this mindset can lead to excessive responsibility and stress, which in the long run can hinder our well-being and our ability to focus on the things that matter most. Delegating tasks whenever possible is an effective way to clear mental and physical space in your life. Identify tasks that can be done by other people and entrust them to them. This can include household tasks, work responsibilities, or even small everyday tasks.

Asking for help when you need it is just as important. Don't hesitate to reach out to trusted family, friends or colleagues for support or advice. Everyone has their own skills and resources, and often others are more than willing to lend a hand. This will allow you to share the load and focus on the tasks that need your priority attention. Delegating and asking for help will not only help you simplify your life, but also make meaningful connections with others. Minimalism isn't just about eliminating material things, it's also about creating space for relationships and mutual support. Remember that you are part of a community and that you can count on others to help you on your path to a simpler, more meaningful life.

Learning to delegate and ask for help takes practice and an open mind. Be willing to let go of control and accept support from others. Over time, you will find that this habit will allow you to live a more balanced life, free from stress and focused on the things that truly matter.

Learn to say **"no"** to requests that don't contribute to your main goals. This helps you avoid overloading yourself with unnecessary commitments. . Learning to say "no" to requests that don't contribute to your main goals is essential to avoid overloading yourself with unnecessary commitments. Often, we find ourselves saying "yes" to too many things, fearing disappointing others or missing out on opportunities. However, this attitude can lead to over-commitments that distract us from our goals and leave us little time and space for the things that really matter.

Practicing "no" requires a good deal of self-awareness and clarity about your goals and priorities. Before accepting a request, take the time to consider whether it will contribute to your overall well-being and if it aligns with your main goals.

Ask yourself if that request will bring you joy, satisfaction, or help you progress toward what you truly desire.

Remember that saying "no" doesn't mean being selfish or insensitive, but rather being aware of your limitations and needs. Learning to set healthy boundaries and protect your time and energy will allow you to focus on the activities that are truly important to you.

Knowing how to say "no" may take practice and courage, but it will get easier over time. Remember that you have the right to take care of yourself and to spend time on the things that bring you joy and fulfillment. Don't be afraid to say "no" when it feels like it's right for you.

Free yourself from the burden of unnecessary commitments and live a life that is simpler, more meaningful and aligned with your deepest values.

Plan your tasks efficiently, using tools like to-do lists and calendars. This allows you to focus on what you need to do without feeling overwhelmed. Time management is a key element to embracing minimalism and living a simpler, more meaningful life. Planning your tasks efficiently helps you stay focused on what you need to do without feeling overwhelmed.

A useful tool for managing time is creating to-do lists. Take the time to write a list of tasks you need to do, breaking them down into priority and less urgent tasks. This gives you a clear view of your responsibilities and helps you prioritize based on importance and urgency.

Using a calendar can be extremely helpful in organizing your days and weeks. Allocate a specific time to each activity and commitment, taking into account your priorities. Remember to leave room for rest and leisure so you don't overextend yourself.

When planning, try to be realistic about how long it will take to complete tasks. We often tend to overestimate our ability to get many things done in a short time, which can lead to stress and frustration. Be kind to yourself and give yourself time to do tasks accurately and unhurriedly, and remember that time management is not just about organizing tasks, it's also about creating blank spaces in your day. Allowing moments of pause and reflection allows you to recharge your energy and maintain a balanced perspective.

Things can change and unexpected events can arise. Accept that not everything will always go to plan and be willing to make adjustments when necessary. Flexibility will help you stay calm and handle situations more effectively.

Simplify your life by automating repetitive processes, such as monthly payments or reminders. Another key tenet of minimalism is process automation. Simplifying your life by automating repetitive processes saves you time and energy, freeing up mental space for what matters most.

One way to automate your life is to set up automatic monthly payments for utility bills or other recurring expenses. That way, you won't have to worry about remembering due dates or manually making payments every month. You can also use online payment services or apps to manage your finances more efficiently.

You can automate reminders using apps or digital tools. For example, you can set reminders for appointments, deadlines, or daily tasks. This way, you won't have to depend on your memory or paper to-do lists, but you will have a system that automatically reminds you what you need to do.

Process automation not only makes your life easier, but it also allows you to reduce the stress and anxiety associated with managing repetitive tasks. Freeing yourself from these responsibilities allows you to focus on more meaningful and rewarding activities. However, it's important to remember to strike a balance between automation and mindful presence in your life. Don't let automation become a way to avoid facing your responsibilities or losing touch with the present moment.

Use automation as a tool to simplify your life, but always maintain an active awareness of your actions and choices.

Automating repetitive processes saves you time and lets you focus on what's really important to you. Take advantage of the technology and tools available to simplify your life and live more intentionally and meaningfully.

Make time for activities that take your mind off your daily grind, like art, reading, or music. This can stimulate creativity and relaxation. Creativity and relaxation are two important elements for well-being and happiness in life. Here are some tips for growing both:

- **Find a creative activity you're passionate about**: This could be drawing, painting, writing, music, dance, or any other form of artistic expression. Make regular time for this activity and let your creativity run wild.
- **Explore New Experiences**: Try something new that challenges and inspires you. You could take a cooking class, learn to play a musical instrument, or try a new art form. Let yourself be guided by curiosity and the desire to experiment.
- **Take time to relax**: Find activities that help you relax and rejuvenate. You could practice meditation, do yoga, take a walk in nature, or take up a hobby that relaxes you, like gardening or reading.

- **Create a Space Dedicated to Creativity**: Find a place in your home or workplace where you can engage in creative pursuits and relaxation. Make sure it's a quiet, comfortable place where you can focus and let your creativity flow.
- **Take Regular Breaks**: Take breaks throughout the day to relax and rejuvenate. This can mean taking a short walk, listening to some relaxing music, or simply closing your eyes and breathing deeply for a few minutes.

Remember that creativity and relaxation are personal, so look for what works best for you and make room in your life to cultivate them.

Free yourself from the
bondage of things and
find joy in freedom.

Chapter 4: Relationships and Minimalist Communication

Developing genuine connections requires conscious effort. Focus on those who share your values, as investing in quality relationships promotes happiness and satisfaction. In the context of minimalism, cultivating meaningful relationships becomes even more important. Focusing on those who share your values allows you to make deep and authentic connections. This involves a conscious commitment to devote your time and energy to people who align with your principles and life goals.

Investing in quality relationships promotes happiness and satisfaction because it allows us to feel understood, supported and accepted for who we really are. Authentic relationships offer us a sense of belonging and help us grow and develop as individuals.

In pursuing a minimalist lifestyle, it's important to make a conscious selection of the people with whom we choose to share our time and energy. This doesn't necessarily mean completely excluding people who don't share our values, but rather putting the emphasis on relationships that enrich us and support us on our minimalist path.

Cultivating meaningful relationships requires commitment and dedication, but the resulting benefits are invaluable. Quality relationships offer us emotional support, inspire us, and motivate us to pursue our goals. They also help us stay consistent with our values and live a more authentic and fulfilling life.

Trivial conversations and drama can weigh down communication. To keep it simple, favor meaningful dialogue and don't participate in empty conversations. Eliminating noise in interpersonal communication is a crucial aspect of minimalism. Often times, idle conversations and pointless drama can weigh down our relationships and distract us from the true goals and values we desire to pursue. To simplify our lives and prioritize what is truly important, it is essential to make an informed selection of the conversations in which we participate. We must learn to recognize when a conversation is not adding value to our lives and have the courage to distance ourselves from it.

We should focus on meaningful dialogues, which enrich us intellectually and emotionally. These can cover topics we are passionate about, share personal experiences, discuss ideas and projects that inspire us. In this way, communication becomes a tool for creating deeper and more meaningful connections with others.

Eliminating the noise in interpersonal communication also requires being aware of our words and how we use them. We must avoid falling into the trap of empty conversation, such as gossip or pointless chatter. Instead, we should try to communicate clearly, authentically, and respectfully, listening carefully to others and responding meaningfully.

Dare to say "no" when needed, and communicate your limitations in a respectful way. This fosters mutual respect and reduces mismatched expectations. Communicating clearly is essential to a minimalist life. Often, we find ourselves trapped in relationships or situations that cause us stress and clutter because we are unable to express our needs and wants effectively. Minimalism invites us to be honest with ourselves and with others, to openly communicate what makes us feel uncomfortable or what we need to live a simpler and more meaningful life.

When we learn to communicate clearly, we avoid misunderstandings and misunderstandings, creating spaces for open and sincere dialogue. This allows us to establish more authentic and deeper relationships, based on mutual understanding and mutual respect.

Setting healthy boundaries and communicating clearly takes courage and determination. We may fear disappointing others or being judged, but it's important to remember that our own happiness and well-being are paramount.

Active listening is crucial. Focus on the speaker, ask clarifying questions, and demonstrate genuine interest. This favors a constructive dialogue. Communicating in an authentic and respectful way favors a constructive dialogue in relationships. When we are honest and open about our thoughts, feelings, and needs, we create a space where both parties feel free to express themselves without fear of judgment or negative reactions.

Constructive dialogue also involves actively listening to the other person, trying to understand their point of view and experiences. This requires empathy and open-mindedness, allowing you to overcome any conflicts or misunderstandings.

Communicating authentically and respectfully helps us build relationships based on mutual trust and understanding. It allows us to approach problems collaboratively, seeking solutions that satisfy both parties.

Strive to communicate without judgment. Respect different opinions without criticism. This fosters openness and understanding. Communicating without judging is a fundamental element in the path towards minimalism. When we strive to communicate without prejudice or criticism, a space of openness and mutual understanding is created.

Respect opinions that differ from yours and accept them. This doesn't mean that we have to agree on everything, but rather that we can express our opinions respectfully and listen to the opinions of others without judgment.

In the context of minimalism, communicating without judging allows us to create more authentic and meaningful relationships.

Focus on the interaction, limiting distractions like the phone. You will provide genuine attention. Focusing on interaction and limiting distractions is an essential aspect of minimalism. Often, we are immersed in a sea of distractions that prevent us from living in the present moment and fully connecting with others. A major source of distraction is the telephone, which can disrupt interaction and reduce the genuine attention we can provide.

To practice minimalism in communication, it's important to limit your phone use when interacting with others. Put your phone aside or put it on silent mode to avoid being distracted by notifications or messages. Instead, focus on interacting and actively listening, offering genuine, distraction-free attention.

Limiting distractions is not just about the phone, but other sources of interruptions like television, social media, or other activities that can divert our attention. When we are present in the moment and focus on interacting, we are able to make deeper and more meaningful connections with others.

Find moments of inner calm and in these moments learn to distinguish the essential from the non-essential.

Chapter 5: Embracing Conscious Consumption

Evaluating true needs is a fundamental step on the path to minimalism. Before proceeding with a purchase, it is important to stop for a moment and reflect on whether the object in question is truly indispensable for one's life. Asking yourself whether it's a real need or a superficial desire can help you avoid impulse buying and focus only on what's truly meaningful.

A useful question to ask yourself is, "Will this item really improve my life?" We often find ourselves buying things that we think will make us happier or more satisfied, but in reality they just end up taking up space and piling up over time. Considering the impact a purchase will have on our lives in the long run allows us to make more informed and thoughtful choices.

It is important to evaluate the usefulness of the object you wish to purchase. Asking yourself if it will be really useful in everyday life or if it will just end up being forgotten or replaced in the short term can help you avoid unnecessary waste and accumulation. Minimalism is based on the philosophy of owning only what is essential and which brings us value, so it is essential to carefully select what enters our lives.

Finally, one aspect to consider is the environmental impact of the purchase. Asking yourself if the object is sustainable, if it is made with eco-friendly materials or if it contributes to a more sustainable lifestyle can be a further evaluation criterion. Minimalism is not only about reducing the superfluous, but also about being aware of our actions and the consequences they can have on the surrounding environment.

Before making a purchase, it's important to take the time to do thorough research. Reading reviews, comparing available options, and evaluating product efficacy, quality, and ethics are all key to making informed decisions.

Reading reviews from other buyers can provide valuable insights into personal experiences with the product. This can help you understand if the item will meet your expectations and if it will be really useful in the long run. Furthermore, comparing the different options available on the market allows you to evaluate the features and prices, helping you to make an informed choice.

In addition to the effectiveness and quality of the product, it is also important to consider the ethics of the brand or company that produces it. Finding out about production practices, the use of sustainable materials and corporate social responsibility can help you make a choice in line with the values of minimalism. Choosing products from companies that are committed to sustainability and ethics can help reduce the environmental and social impact of our purchases.

Research and information are powerful tools to avoid impulsive purchases and to select only what is really necessary. Investing time in product research allows us to make informed choices, reducing waste and concentrating our resources on what is truly meaningful to us.

We are often faced with temptations to buy items that seem appealing, but may actually not be necessary or in line with our minimalist values. To counteract this urge, it's important to pause before making a purchase.

Taking time to reflect is an effective way to assess whether the product is really necessary in our lives. Before making a purchase, take a moment to ask yourself if the item will satisfy a real need or if it's just a momentary desire. Ask yourself if the purchase will help improve your life significantly or if it will just end up taking up space and accumulating over time.

During this pause for thought, it's also important to consider whether the product matches your minimalist values. Ask yourself if the object is in line with the philosophy of owning only what is essential and which adds value to your life. Consider whether the purchase aligns with your quest for a more sustainable, ethical, and mindful lifestyle. This rating will help you make more informed decisions and avoid purchases that might go against your minimalist goals.

Furthermore, during the pause for reflection, you can also evaluate if there are alternatives to the product you are considering. You may find that there are simpler, cheaper or more sustainable solutions that can meet your needs without having to buy something new.

On the path to a minimalist lifestyle, it is essential to choose products that have a reduced environmental impact. Looking for sustainable and eco-friendly options not only allows us to reduce our impact on the environment, but also contributes to the protection of the planet for future generations. When it comes to shopping, it's important to consider the product lifecycle. This means evaluating not only the environmental impact during the production phase, but also during use and disposal. Choosing products made with recyclable, biodegradable or sustainably sourced materials can help reduce your overall environmental impact.

It is important to pay attention to the production practices of companies. Look for brands and manufacturers that adopt sustainable policies, such as the use of renewable energy, reducing carbon emissions and respecting workers' rights. This will allow you to make informed choices and support companies that are committed to environmental protection.

Another aspect to consider is the durability of the product. Choosing quality products that are built to last over time reduces the need to replace them frequently and helps reduce waste. Opting for products that can be repaired or recycled, rather than thrown away, is an effective way to reduce your overall environmental impact

Reducing waste and adopting a sustainable lifestyle are fundamental pillars of minimalism. One of the key strategies to achieve this is the reuse and recycling of the items we already own. Instead of rushing to buy something new, it's important to try to make the most of what we already have.

Reuse is an effective way to breathe new life into objects that might be considered superfluous. Rather than throwing something away, ask yourself if it can be reused in another way or if it can be given to someone else who needs it. For example, old clothes can be turned into new clothing or donated to charities. Furniture or household items can be repaired or refurbished rather than replaced.

Creative recycling is another strategy that can reduce waste. Rather than throwing away materials like paper, plastic or glass, try to find ways to reuse them in creative ways. For example, mason jars can become food containers or plant pots, while old magazines can be used to create artwork or decorations. Furthermore, it is important to adopt a sustainable lifestyle in everyday life. This means making conscious choices to reduce resource use and environmental impact. For example, reducing the consumption of single-use plastics, preferring products with minimal or recyclable packaging and using renewable energy sources are all actions that contribute to a more sustainable lifestyle.

Choose products with minimal or recyclable packaging. This reduces rejection and promotes a low-impact lifestyle.

Before buying something new, it's important to consider whether you can get rid of a similar item you already own, thus maintaining a balance in the number of items you own.

This practice helps you avoid hoarding and keep only what is essential in your life. Before making a new purchase, ask yourself if you already have a similar item that can perform the same function. If so, consider deleting the old item to make room for the new one. This allows you to maintain balance and avoid piling up unnecessary items.

The practice of "One In, One Out" also helps you reflect on the real value of what you own.

Ask yourself if the item you are considering buying is really necessary and if it will add value to your life. If you can't identify an item that you can discard to make room for the new one, it could be a sign that the purchase isn't really necessary.

Additionally, this practice encourages you to be more aware of your purchasing choices. It pushes you to carefully consider whether the object you wish to purchase is truly meaningful to you and whether it matches your minimalist values.

Instead of purchasing items that might only be used occasionally, consider sharing them with friends or family. This reduces the need to own everything individually and promotes a spirit of collaboration and sharing.

Sharing the occasional item with people around you has several benefits. First, it allows you to save money by avoiding the purchase of items that you may only rarely use. It also reduces the accumulation of items in your home, helping to maintain a tidier, clutter-free space.

Sharing and lending items can happen in several ways. You can set up trades with friends or family, where each person contributes items that can be used by others for a set amount of time.

You may also consider joining online groups or communities that promote sharing of items, such as tools, appliances, or sports equipment.
This practice not only reduces the environmental impact by avoiding the production and purchase of useless objects, but also promotes a sense of community and solidarity. Sharing objects with others creates stronger social bonds and favors a more sustainable and conscious lifestyle. Embracing mindful consumption involves making thoughtful choices that reflect your values and promote a sustainable lifestyle.

It's the essential that satisfies the soul and not the superfluous

Chapter 6: Minimalism in Personal Care

In the hectic world we live in, dedicating time to personal care becomes essential for our well-being. However, minimalism invites us to reflect on how we can simplify this sphere of our lives as well, creating an essential and rewarding self-care routine.

One of the first challenges we encounter in pursuing minimalist self-care is the information overload in the wellness industry. We are bombarded with ads, tips and products that promise to improve our beauty and well-being. However, minimalism invites us to make a conscious selection of what we really need.

Eliminating information overload means filtering information sources, choosing only those that reflect our values and needs.

Instead of following all the latest trends and products, we can focus on what works for us, creating a personal care routine that is authentic and meaningful.

Another important aspect of minimalism in personal care is the pursuit of natural and authentic beauty. We are often led to believe that we have to follow unrealistic beauty standards and spend a fortune on cosmetic products and beauty treatments. However, minimalism invites us to reflect on what it really means to be beautiful.

It means accepting and loving ourselves for who we are, embracing our uniqueness and authenticity.

We can pursue natural beauty through personal care based on simple and sustainable products, favoring natural and organic ingredients. Instead of hiding our imperfections, we can learn to appreciate them as part of our history and unique beauty. Creating an essential and rewarding self-care routine is one way to make time consciously and meaningfully. Here are some steps to create a minimalist self-care routine:

- Simplicity in the choice of products: Choose a few quality products that meet your specific needs. Avoid the accumulation of useless objects and favor natural and organic ingredients. For example, you might opt for a gentle face wash, a light moisturizer, and a natural body oil.

- **Quiet moments**: Take time each day to relax and rejuvenate. You can practice meditation, take a walk in nature or simply enjoy a moment of silence and calm. These moments of tranquility will help you reduce stress and find inner balance.

- **Conscious movement**: Include physical activities in your routine that you enjoy and that make you feel good. You could practice yoga, go for a walk, or do some stretching exercises. The important thing is to choose an activity that allows you to connect with your body and enjoy the movement.

- **Healthy Nutrition**: Take care of your body through a balanced and healthy diet. Choose fresh and nutritious foods, favoring fruits, vegetables, whole grains and lean proteins. Avoid processed foods and foods high in added sugar. Remember that food is a way of nourishing your body and providing it with the energy it needs.

- **Moments of Pleasure**: Spend time doing what you enjoy and makes you feel good. You could read a book, listen to music, paint, or take a walk in the park. The important thing is to give yourself moments of pleasure that allow you to detach from the routine and enjoy the present.

- **Quality sleep**: Make sure you have a good sleep routine. Try to go to bed and wake up at the same times each day, creating a routine that is conducive to rest and recovery. Make sure you have a quiet, comfortable sleeping environment and get at least 7-8 hours of sleep each night.

Minimalism does **NOT** mean that you don't have to own anything, but that nothing should own you

Chapter 7: Minimalism in Work and Career

Minimalism can also be applied in the workplace, allowing you to improve efficiency and personal well-being. In this chapter, we'll explore how to leverage the minimalist approach to achieve greater productivity and find meaning in your career path.

- Simplicity in organization: Simplifying work organization is essential to improve efficiency. Minimize distractions and focus on activities that bring value. Use digital or physical tools that help you keep track of tasks and deadlines in a clear and orderly way. Eliminate unnecessary items from your desk or workspace, creating a clean and tidy environment that encourages concentration.

- Prioritize and Delegate: Identify the most important and urgent tasks and focus on them. Learn to delegate tasks that are not essential or can be done by other people. Minimalism at work means focusing on activities that require your skills and bring value, while leaving room for leisure and personal well-being.

- Balance between productivity and well-being: Minimalism in work is not only about being more productive, but also about finding a balance between work and personal well-being. Make time for yourself, your family, and activities that bring you joy and satisfaction outside of work. Set clear boundaries between work time and free time, avoiding letting work invade every aspect of your life.

- Finding Meaning in Work: Minimalism in work also involves finding meaning in one's career path. Reflect on what you are passionate about and how you can contribute your skills and talents. Try to align your work with your personal values and goals, so that you feel accomplished and fulfilled. If necessary, consider making changes in your career to pursue a more meaningful path.

- Stress Reduction: Minimalism in your work can help you reduce stress and improve your overall well-being. Eliminate activities or commitments that cause you stress and are not essential to your job. Learn to say no when necessary and set healthy boundaries to protect your mental and physical health.

- Flexibility and adaptability: Minimalism in work also requires flexibility and adaptability. Be open to change and the possibility of experimenting with new ways of working. Embrace the idea of doing less, but better, focusing on the quality of your activities and your results.

Chapter 8: Food and waste reduction

In the previous chapter we explored how minimalism can be applied in different aspects of our lives, including work and career. In this chapter, we'll focus on applying minimalism to food and cooking, discovering how to take a minimalist approach to reducing food waste and embracing a simpler diet.

A minimalist approach to nutrition begins with making a conscious choice of the foods we consume. Choose fresh, unprocessed and seasonal foods. Avoid foods with artificial ingredients or overpackaged foods. Focus on nutritious foods that provide you with energy and essential nutrients. Opt for fresh fruits and vegetables, whole grains, lean proteins, and sources of healthy fats like avocados and nuts.

Minimize your intake of added sugars, saturated fats, and salt.

Remember that food is a way of nourishing your body and providing it with what it needs to function at its best. Choosing simple, nutritious foods will help you maintain a balanced diet and reduce the accumulation of unnecessary foods in your pantry.

Reduction of food waste: Minimalism in nutrition also implies the reduction of waste. Plan meals in advance and make a shopping list to buy only what you need. Use leftovers to make new dishes or freeze them for future use. Be aware of the portions you prepare and try not to waste food.

Here is a list of ingredients you can use.

Vegetables:
- Carrots
- Celery
- Onions
- Tomatoes
- Peppers

Proteins:
- Chicken
- Beef
- Fish
- Egg

Carbohydrates:
- Rice
- Pasta
- Bread

Dairy products:
- Cheese
- Milk
- Yogurt

Spices and condiments:

- salt
- Pepper
- Olive oil
- Vinegar
- Soy sauce

In addition to these ingredients, make sure you have doggy storage containers and freezer bags. When preparing meals, try to use leftovers creatively. For example, you can make chicken soup with leftover roast chicken, or you can use leftover veggies to make an omelet. Freeze leftovers that you can't consume right away for future use.

Here are some tips for minimizing the kitchen.

- Kitchen Essentials: Simplify your kitchen by cutting down on appliances and utensils you don't use. Keep only the essential tools to prepare your meals. Minimize the number of pots, pans and containers you own. This will help you maintain a tidy and functional kitchen environment.

- Home cooking: You prefer to cook your own meals at home instead of eating out or ordering take out. Home cooking allows you to control the ingredients you use and avoid excess packaging and additives. Plus, cooking at home can be a rewarding and relaxing experience.

- Simplicity in presentation: You don't have to create elaborate or complicated dishes to enjoy a tasty meal. Simplicity in the presentation of dishes can be equally appreciated. Focus on the quality of the ingredients and their harmonious combination. Get creative with spices and herbs to add flavor without weighing down the dish. Using spices and herbs is a great way to add flavor to dishes without weighing them down.

- Here are some tips for getting creative with spices and herbs:

Experiment with Spices: Explore a variety of spices such as turmeric, cumin, paprika, black pepper, cinnamon, ginger, nutmeg, and cardamom. Each spice has a unique flavor and can transform a simple dish into something special.

- Use fresh herbs: Fresh herbs such as basil, parsley, cilantro, thyme, rosemary and mint can add a touch of freshness to your dishes. Add them at the end of the preparation to preserve their flavor and aroma.

- Create Custom Spice Blends: You can create your own custom spice blends by combining different spices according to your taste. For example, you can create a spice blend for meat, fish or vegetables.

- Add Spices to Sauces and Marinades: Spices can be used to spice up sauces and marinades. For example, you can add smoked paprika to a barbecue sauce or ginger and garlic to a chicken marinade.

- Balance Flavors: Remember to balance the flavors of spices and herbs to achieve a harmonious result. Make sure that no spice or herb overpowers the other ingredients.

- Experiment with International Cuisines: Explore the cuisines of different cultures to discover new spices and herb combinations. For example, Indian cuisine, Mexican cuisine, and Mediterranean cuisine offer a wide range of spices and herbs to use.

- Mindfulness during meals: Eat slowly and mindfully, enjoying every bite. Avoid distractions like television or cell phones during meals, instead focusing on the pleasure of nourishing your body.

Minimalism is a journey towards simplicity, where less becomes more and what's left is what really matters.

Chapter 9: Minimalism, Authenticity and Minimalism in Luxury

Minimalism is much more than a simple lifestyle based on the reduction of material objects. It can also be a powerful tool for discovering one's authenticity and pursuing one's self-actualization. When we let go of the excesses and distractions in our lives, we are able to focus on what is truly important to us. Minimalism invites us to make a deep reflection on what makes us truly happy and satisfied. It encourages us to explore our values, interests, and passions, and to purge anything that doesn't resonate with our authenticity. This process of self-exploration can be liberating and allows us to live lives that are more aligned with who we truly are.

When we get rid of superfluous objects and activities that don't satisfy us, we create space for what really makes us happy. We can spend more time and energy on people we love, activities we are passionate about, and projects that excite us. Minimalism helps us focus on meaningful experiences and create a more authentic and fulfilling life. Furthermore, minimalism invites us to reflect on our impact on the world around us. It pushes us to consider our consumption choices and to reduce the environmental impact of our actions. This allows us to live in harmony with nature and contribute to a more sustainable world.

Minimalism gives us a space to explore our authenticity, to focus on what's truly important to us, and to live a life aligned with our values.

It is a path that requires reflection, awareness and courage, but can lead us to a more authentic, satisfying and meaningful life.

Minimalism in luxury is an intriguing concept that invites us to reevaluate our definition of what is truly precious and valuable.

Having explored the link between minimalism and authenticity, we can also apply these principles to the way we perceive and experience luxury.

We often associate the concept of luxury with expensive, exclusive and branded items. However, minimalism in luxury challenges us to look at luxury differently. It's about appreciating things of value, but without falling into excessive hoarding or the desire to always possess more.

Minimalist luxury is based on quality rather than quantity. It means choosing objects that are well made, long lasting and that bring significant value to our lives. Instead of filling our home with superfluous luxury items, we focus on a select few pieces that bring us joy and satisfaction.

Minimalist luxury also extends to the experience. It means indulging in moments of relaxation and pleasure, such as a walk in nature, a dinner with friends or a quiet evening reading a good book. These precious and authentic moments become our personal luxury, which does not necessarily require a large financial investment.

Minimalist luxury also invites us to consider the impact of our choices on the planet and the people who inhabit it.

It pushes us to look for sustainable and ethical options, such as products made with recycled or responsibly sourced materials. This way, we can enjoy luxury without contributing to overconsumption and negative impacts on the environment.

To embrace minimalist luxury, it's important to think consciously about our priorities and values. Let's ask ourselves what is truly important to us and how we can integrate luxury into our lives in a meaningful way. We can choose to invest in experiences rather than possessions, to cultivate meaningful relationships, and to appreciate the little things that bring us joy.

Minimalism gives us the freedom to focus on the experiences, relationships and passions that truly enrich us.

Chapter 10: Minimalism and Decision-Making

Making conscious and simple decisions is a key element of minimalism. In the previous chapter we explored the concept of minimalist luxury and how to apply it to our lives. In this chapter, we will explore how minimalism can influence our decision making in every aspect of life.

Before making a decision, it's important to identify your core values. Ask yourself what are the things that are really important to you in life and what your long-term goals are. This will help you make decisions that are aligned with what is truly meaningful to you.

Minimalism invites us to simplify our choices. Avoid overloading yourself with options and consider only those that are essential to you. Minimize distractions and outside influences that can confuse your decision making.

When making a decision, focus your attention on the essentials. Ask yourself what things are truly necessary and meaningful in that situation. Avoid complicating things with superfluous details and only consider what is truly relevant to your decision.

Minimalism invites us to consider the long-term consequences of our decisions. Ask yourself how a certain choice might affect your life in the long run. Try to avoid impulsive decisions that could lead to unwanted consequences in the future.

Ask yourself if a particular choice is in line with your priorities and if it brings you closer to your goals. Be willing to say "no" to what's not aligned with what's truly important to you. Take the time to connect with yourself and listen to what your inner voice is telling you. Often, our intuition knows which decision is best for us, even though it may seem counterintuitive.

Strategies to avoid overanalysis and overcomplication:

- **Simplicity in selection**: When it comes to choosing valuables, it is important to avoid excessive hoarding. Focus on a few high quality items that bring you joy and satisfaction. Avoid falling into the trap of "more is better" and carefully choose what adds value to your life.

- **Evaluate functionality**: Before buying a luxury item, carefully evaluate its functionality. Ask yourself if the item satisfies a real need in your life or if it's just a passing desire. Focus on items that offer you practical value and can be used regularly.

- **Quality over quantity**: Choose quality over quantity. Invest in luxury items that are made with fine materials and excellent craftsmanship. These items will last over time and give you greater satisfaction than a series of low quality items.

- **Avoid ephemeral trends**: Trends come and go, but minimalism focuses on durability. Avoid falling into the trap of fads and instead choose items that have a timeless style. This will allow you to enjoy them for a long time without having to constantly replace them.

- **Limit Information Sources**: The digital age gives us a huge amount of information and advertising which can lead to an overload of choices. Limit your sources of information, choosing only those that reflect your values and your needs.

- **Create an essential self-care routine**: Focus on taking care of yourself in an essential and rewarding way. Avoid overcomplicating your personal care routine with unnecessary products and treatments. Choose a few high-quality products that meet your needs and make you feel good.

- **Be aware of your motivations**: Before making a luxury purchase, reflect on your motivations. Ask yourself if you are trying to fill an emotional void or trying to impress others. Be honest with yourself and make choices that reflect your true wants and needs.

- Focus on the experience: Minimalism isn't just limited to material objects. Focus on the experience and significant relationships in your life. Invest your time and resources in activities that bring you joy and enrich your life, such as travel, hobbies, or spending time with loved ones.

- Be flexible: Minimalism in luxury is not a rigid formula, but rather a flexible approach to life. Be open to exploring new ideas and adapting your lifestyle to your ever-changing needs. Don't be afraid to make changes and discard what no longer serves you.

Minimalism reminds us that our true wealth lies in experiences, relationships and connection with the world around us.

Chapter 11: Minimalism in Education

The values of minimalism can be taught to children in a fun and easy way, without the need for lengthy introductions. In this chapter, we'll explore some practical strategies for introducing the principles of minimalism into children's lives.

Game of "Reduce and Recycle": Organize a special day where you involve your children in the game of "Reduce and Recycle". Ask them to sort out toys, clothes, or items they no longer use, and explain to them the importance of donating or recycling what you don't need. Teach them to make informed choices and reduce the accumulation of useless items.

Experiences instead of things: Teaching children to value experiences rather than material objects is a fundamental aspect of minimalism. Organize activities that promote creativity, such as painting, reading, or playing outside. Teach them that experiences can bring more lasting joy and satisfaction than buying new things.

Order and cleanliness: Minimalism is based on the idea of keeping a space neat and clean. Involve your children in creating a tidy environment, teaching them to put away toys after playing and to keep their room tidy. Explain to them that a tidy environment can promote concentration and calmness.

Giving and Sharing: Teaching children the value of sharing and giving is an important aspect of minimalism.

Organize a collection of toys, clothes or books together with your children to donate to those in need. Explain to them that giving away what they no longer use can bring happiness to other people and reduce the accumulation of unused items.

Appreciate what you have: Teach your children to be grateful for what they have. Every day, encourage them to reflect on what makes them happy and to express gratitude for the little things. This will help them develop an abundance mindset and understand that happiness does not depend on material objects.

Limit media exposure: Minimalism focuses on the essentials and reducing background noise. Limit the time your children spend in front of the television or electronic devices. Teach them to enjoy silence, nature, and screen-free activities.

Simplicity of choice: Teaching children to make informed choices is a key aspect of minimalism. Help them understand that it is not necessary to have everything they want. Teach them to carefully evaluate their needs and make choices based on quality and functionality, rather than quantity.

Promoting meaningful learning and awareness is vital in helping children develop a deep and lasting understanding of concepts. Below are some strategies that can be used to achieve this:

- **Connect new concepts to personal experience**: To make learning meaningful, it is important to connect new concepts to children's personal experience. Ask them to reflect on situations or experiences where they can apply the concepts they are learning. For example, if they're learning about sustainability, ask them to think of ways they can reduce the use of plastic in their daily lives.

- **Encourage active learning**: Active learning engages children in hands-on activities that put them at the center of the learning process. For example, instead of just reading a book, ask them to participate in discussions, do research, or create projects that require applying the concepts they learn. This type of active engagement helps children better understand concepts and develop deeper awareness.

- **Use Critical Thinking**: Teaching children to think critically is an effective way to promote meaningful learning. Ask them to analyze information, ask questions, and evaluate evidence to support an idea. Teach them to consider different perspectives and form opinions based on logical reasoning.

- **Making Connections Between Concepts**: Helps children make connections between the concepts they are learning. Show them how the concepts relate to each other and how they can be applied in different situations. For example, if they're learning about cultural diversity, ask them to think about how diversity can affect relationships, art, or music. These kinds of connections help children develop a broader understanding and deeper awareness of concepts.

- **Promote reflection and self-reflection**: Ask children to reflect on their learning and evaluate the progress they have made. Teach them to ask questions about what they learned, how they applied it, and how they could improve. This type of reflection and self-reflection helps children develop a critical awareness of their learning processes and identify areas where they can further grow.

Simplicity is the key to clearing your mind of chaos and finding inner peace.

Chapter 12: Inner journey and search for the self

The inner journey is a personal and profound experience that allows us to explore our most authentic self. When we apply the principles of minimalism to this path, we can discover greater clarity, serenity, and awareness. In this chapter, we'll explore how minimalism can enrich our inner journey without unnecessary distractions.

On the inner journey, it is important to simplify our practices to focus on the essentials. Rather than trying to follow multiple techniques or philosophies, we pick one or two practices that resonate with us and delve into them.

It could be meditation, daily writing, or practicing silence. By reducing the number of practices, we can devote more time and energy to each one, allowing them to deepen and have a more significant impact on our inner journey.

Minimalism teaches us to get rid of material attachments, but it can also be applied to emotional and mental attachments. On the inner journey, we try to acknowledge and let go of attachments that we hold onto, such as expectations, limiting beliefs, or toxic relationships. This allows us to create space for new experiences and for greater inner freedom.

In the inner journey, the relationships we cultivate are fundamental. We apply the principle of minimalism to our relationships, seeking to cultivate those that are authentic, meaningful, and nurturing. This means being selective in our connections and dedicating our time and energy to those who support and inspire us. By reducing superficial or toxic relationships, we can create a space for deeper and more meaningful connections, inviting us to find moments of silence and solitude. We create spaces in our day for reflection, meditation, or simple inner stillness. These moments allow us to connect with our deeper self, to hear our inner voice, and to develop greater self-awareness.

Minimalism teaches us to live in the present, without being tied to the past or worried about the future. In the inner journey, we try to apply this awareness to the present moment. We experience the joy and beauty of the present moment, without being distracted by thoughts or worries. This practice helps us develop greater mindfulness and connect with our inner experience in a deeper way, we learn to be grateful for what we have and to appreciate the little things. We apply this awareness to our inner journey, recognizing and appreciating the progress we make, the lessons we learn, and the experiences that enrich us. Gratitude helps us maintain a positive outlook and cultivate a greater awareness of our inner journey.

Here are some tips for cultivating gratitude:

Keep a Gratitude Journal: Take time each day to write down at least three things you are grateful for. It could be little things like a stunning sunset, a hot cup of coffee, or a chat with a friend. Or it could be bigger things like health, meaningful relationships, or the opportunities you have in life. Writing these things down helps you focus on the blessings you have and develop a positive outlook.

Express gratitude to others: Take the time to thank the people you care about. You can do this through a thank you message, a phone call or even a simple hug. Showing gratitude to others not only makes them feel appreciated, but it also helps you recognize the importance of relationships in your life. Pause to appreciate the present moment: From time to time, stop and observe your surroundings. Become aware of the small details that often go unnoticed. It can be the scent of flowers, the sound of birds or the feel of the sun on your skin. Appreciating the present moment helps you live in the here and now and recognize the beauty around you.

Practice self-compassion: Be kind to yourself and acknowledge your successes and positive qualities. Don't just focus on the negatives or things you would like to improve. Accept yourself for who you are and appreciate your uniqueness.

Exploring **the path of the self through** a minimalist lens invites us to reflect on the search for meaning, purpose and inner connection in a more intentional and mindful way. Minimalism challenges us to carefully examine what we consider essential in our lives and to rid ourselves of anything that distracts us from our true purpose. It encourages us to ask deep questions about the meaning of our existence and to seek answers within ourselves, rather than seeking them in material things or external success. Through practicing minimalism in the inner journey, we can discover that meaning and purpose are not something to be achieved or achieved, but rather something to be cultivated and experienced in the present moment.

It invites us to explore our deepest passions, values, and aspirations, and to create a space in our lives to pursue them with authenticity and integrity.

Minimalism in the inner journey also prompts us to examine our relationships and to cultivate meaningful connections. It encourages us to shed the toxic or superficial relationships that drag us down and focus on the ones that nourish and sustain us. Through the practice of minimalism in relationships, we can create a space for deep and authentic connections, where we can share experiences, emotions and thoughts openly and sincerely.

We learn to slow down and find moments of silence and solitude.

These quiet moments allow us to connect with our deeper self, to hear our inner voice, and to develop greater self-awareness. They help us reflect on our experiences, better understand our desires, and identify what brings us joy and genuine satisfaction.

Through the practice of minimalism in the inner journey, we can discover that the search for meaning, purpose and inner connection is not a goal to reach, but rather an ongoing process of exploration and discovery. It invites us to live more mindfully, to embrace simplicity and to cultivate greater gratitude for the little things. In this way, we can create a clearer and more serene inner space in which we can cultivate a deeper connection with ourselves, with others and with the world around us.

Awareness connects us
to the depths of life,
makes us appreciate the
beauty and fragility of
every moment.

Chapter 13: Daily Life and Conclusions

In this concluding chapter, we want to reflect on the power of minimalism in everyday life and how it can profoundly transform our existence. We have explored different areas where minimalism can be applied, such as home organization, conscious consumption, education and even the inner journey. Each aspect offered a unique perspective on how to simplify, eliminate the redundant and focus on the things that really matter.

Through minimalism, we have learned to free ourselves from material constraints and social expectations, to embrace a more meaningful and authentic lifestyle.

We have discovered that happiness does not lie in the quantity of things we possess, but in the quality of our experiences and relationships.
Minimalism has taught us to reflect on the meaning and purpose of our lives. It prompted us to pause and ask ourselves what really makes us happy and satisfied. Through this soul searching, we have discovered that true meaning lies in the connection with ourselves, with others and with the world around us.
We have learned to cultivate gratitude for the little things, to live in the present moment and to appreciate the beauty of simplicity. We have discovered that our happiness does not depend on what we possess, but on how we live and how we relate to the world.

Minimalism has also taught us to be more aware of our choices and the consequences these can have on the environment and society. We have learned to reduce our ecological footprint, consume responsibly and promote a sustainable lifestyle.

Bottom line, minimalism is so much more than just a lifestyle. It's a philosophical approach that invites us to examine our priorities, eliminate the superfluous and focus on the things that really matter. It offers us the possibility to live a more authentic, meaningful life and in harmony with ourselves and with the world around us. We hope this journey into the world of minimalism has inspired you and given you the tools to embrace a simpler, more fulfilling lifestyle.

Remember that minimalism is not a law, but a personal path that each of us can adapt to our needs and values.
May the power of minimalism continue to guide you towards a life filled with meaning, purpose and inner connection. Have a good trip!

www.ingramcontent.com/pod-product-compliance
Lightning Source LLC
Chambersburg PA
CBHW071325140726
47996CB00005B/1822